John Kember and Graeme Vinall

Saxophone Sight-Reading 1

Déchiffrage pour le saxophone 1
Vom-Blatt-Spiel auf dem Saxophon 1

A fresh approach / Nouvelle approche
Eine erfrischend neue Methode

ED 13053
ISMN M-2201-2625-3
ISBN 978-1-902455-87-7

www.schott-music.com

Mainz · London · Madrid · New York · Paris · Prague · Tokyo · Toronto
© 2007 SCHOTT MUSIC Ltd, London · Printed in Germany

ED 13053

British Library Cataloguing-in-Publication Data.
A catalogue record for this book is available from the British Library.
ISMN M-2201-2625-3
ISBN 978-1-902455-87-7

© 2007 Schott Music Ltd, London

All rights reserved. Printed in Germany. No part of this publication may be reproduced,
stored in a retrieval system, or transmitted, in any form or by any means, electronic,
mechanical, photocopying, recording or otherwise, without the prior written permission of
Schott Music Ltd, 48 Great Marlborough Street, London WlF 7BB

French translation: Agnès Ausseur
German translation: Ute Corleis
Cover design and layout by www.adamhaystudio.com
Music setting and page layout by Jackie Leigh
Printed in Germany S&Co.8280

Contents
Sommaire / Inhalt

Preface

Saxophone Sight-Reading 1 aims to establish good practice and provide an early introduction to the essential skill of sight-reading.

Ideally, sight-reading in some form should be a regular part of a student's routine each time they play their saxophone, both in the practice room and in a lesson.

This book aims to establish the habit early in a student's saxophone playing. Of course, names of notes and time values need to be thoroughly known and understood, but sight-reading is equally helped by an awareness of shape and direction.

There are seven sections in this book, each of which gradually introduces new notes, rhythms, articulations, dynamics and Italian terms in a logical sequence, much as you would find in a beginner's tutor book. The emphasis is on providing idiomatic tunes and structures rather than sterile sight-reading exercises. Each section begins with solo examples and concludes with duets and accompanied pieces, enabling the player to gain experience of sight-reading within the context of ensemble playing.

Solos and duets are suitable for both alto and tenor instruments, and accompanied pieces are given with piano parts to suit each.

Section 1 begins with the notes G to B and gradually extends this to D. Melodic material emphasises movement by step and skip, simple phrase structures, repeated notes and repeated melodic shapes (sequences).

Section 2 extends the range with notes lower E to upper E and introduces F#, slurs and ties.

Section 3 ranges from lower D to upper G and introduces the key signatures of C, G and F major, together with the new notes B♭ and upper F#, quavers (eighth notes), dynamics and performance directions. The ♩. ♪ figure is introduced in simple time signatures 4/4, 3/4 and 2/4.

Section 4 introduces 3/8 time and compound times of 6/8, 9/8 and 12/8. The key of D major is introduced, along with new notes C# and upper A.

Section 5 extends the range to include G# and upper B♭. The time signature of 5/4 is introduced, along with the minor keys of A, D and B minor.

Section 6 concentrates on syncopations and swing rhythms. The keys of B♭ major and E minor are introduced.

Section 7 concludes book 1 with a range of two octaves (lower C to upper C), and the keys of G minor and A major.

To the pupil: why sight-reading?

When you are faced with a new piece and asked to play it, whether at home, in a lesson or in an exam or audition, there is no one to help you – except yourself! Sight-reading tests your ability to read the time and notes correctly, and to observe the phrasing and dynamics quickly.

The aim of this book is to help you to teach yourself. The book gives guidance on what to look for and how best to prepare in a very short time by observing the time and key signatures, the shape of the melody and the marks of expression. These short pieces progress gradually to help you to build up your confidence and observation, and enable you to sight-read accurately. At the end of each section there are duets to play with your teacher or friends, and pieces with piano accompaniment, which will test your ability to sight-read while something else is going on. This is a necessary skill when playing with a band, orchestra or other ensemble.

If you sight-read something every time you play your saxophone you will be amazed how much better you will become. Remember: if you can sight-read most of the tunes you are asked to learn, you will be able to concentrate on the 'tricky bits' and complete them quickly.

Think of the tunes in this book as mini-pieces, and try to learn them quickly and correctly. Then when you are faced with real sight-reading, you will be well-equipped to succeed at the first attempt.

You are on your own now!

Préface

Le propos de ce premier volume de déchiffrage pour le saxophone est de fournir une initiation et un entraînement solide aux principes de la lecture à vue.

L'idéal serait que le déchiffrage, sous une forme ou une autre, prenne régulièrement place dans la routine de travail de l'élève à chaque fois qu'il prend son saxophone pour s'exercer ou pendant une leçon.

L'objectif est ici d'établir l'habitude de la lecture à vue très tôt dans l'étude du saxophone. Le déchiffrage suppose, bien sûr, que les noms et les valeurs de notes soient complètement assimilés et compris mais il s'appuie également sur la reconnaissance des contours et de la direction mélodiques.

Ce volume comporte sept parties dont chacune correspond à l'introduction de notes, de rythmes, de phrasés, de nuances et de termes italiens nouveaux selon la progression logique rencontrée dans une méthode pour débutant. La démarche consiste à fournir des airs et des structures propres au répertoire du saxophone de préférence à de stériles exercices de déchiffrage. Chaque partie débute par plusieurs pièces en solo et se termine par des duos et des pièces accompagnées de manière à familiariser l'instrumentiste avec le déchiffrage collectif.

Les morceaux en solo et les duos sont adaptés aux saxophones alto et ténor. De même, les parties de piano des pièces accompagnées sont fournies pour les deux instruments.

Section 1 – notes *sol* à *si* et extension progressive jusqu'au *ré*. Les mélodies présentent des progressions par degrés conjoints et disjoints, des structures de phrases simples, des notes répétées et des motifs mélodiques répétés (séquences).

Section 2 – extension de la tessiture du *mi* grave au *mi* aigu. Introduction du *fa*♯ des liaisons et liaisons de phrasé.

Section 3 – extension de la tessiture du *ré* grave au *sol* aigu et introduction des armures des tonalités de *do* majeur, *sol* majeur et *fa* majeur, ainsi que des notes *si*♭ et *fa*♯, des croches, de nuances dynamiques et d'indications pour l'exécution. Le rythme ♩. ♪ apparaît dans des mesures simples à 4/4, 3/4 et 2/4.

Section 4 – introduction de la mesure à 3/8 et des mesures composées à 6/8, 9/8 et 12/8, de la tonalité de *ré* majeur, ainsi que des notes *do*♯ et *la* aigu.

Section 5 – extension de la tessiture au *sol*♯ aigu et *si*♭. Introduction de la mesure à 5/4 et des tonalités de *la* mineur, de *ré* mineur et de *si* mineur.

Section 6 – syncopes et rythmique *swing*. Introduction des tonalités de *si*♭ majeur et de *mi*♭ mineur.

Section 7 – conclusion du volume recouvrant une tessiture de deux octaves (*do* grave à *do* aigu) et par les tonalités de *sol* mineur et de *la* majeur.

A l'élève : Pourquoi le déchiffrage ?

Lorsque vous vous trouvez face à un nouveau morceau que l'on vous demande de jouer, que ce soit chez vous, pendant une leçon ou lors d'un examen ou d'une audition, personne d'autre ne peut vous aider que vous-même ! Le déchiffrage met à l'épreuve votre capacité de lecture correcte des rythmes et des notes et d'observation rapide du phrasé et des nuances.

Ce recueil se propose de vous aider à vous entraîner vous-même. Il vous oriente sur ce que vous devez repérer et sur la meilleure manière de vous préparer en un laps de temps très court en sachant relever à la clef les indications de mesure et de tonalité, les contours de la mélodie et les indications expressives. Ces pièces brèves, en progressant par étapes, vous feront prendre de l'assurance, aiguiseront votre sens de l'observation et vous permettront de lire à vue avec exactitude. A la fin de chaque partie figurent des duos que vous pourrez jouer avec votre professeur ou des amis et des morceaux avec accompagnement de piano qui mettront à l'épreuve votre habileté à déchiffrer pendant que se déroule une autre partie. Celle-ci est indispensable pour jouer dans un groupe, un orchestre ou un ensemble.

Vous serez surpris de vos progrès si vous déchiffrez une pièce à chaque fois que vous vous mettez au saxophone. N'oubliez pas que si vous êtes capable de lire à vue la plupart des morceaux que vous allez étudier, vous pourrez vous concentrer sur les passages difficiles et les assimiler plus vite.

Considérez ces pages comme des « mini-morceaux » et essayez de les apprendre rapidement et sans erreur de manière à être bien armé devant un véritable déchiffrage et réussir dès la première lecture.

A vous seul de jouer maintenant !

Vorwort

Vom–Blatt-Spiel auf dem Saxophon 1 möchte zu einer guten Übepraxis verhelfen und frühzeitig für die Einführung der grundlegenden Fähigkeit des Blatt-Spiels sorgen.

Idealerweise sollte das Vom-Blatt-Spiel in irgendeiner Form jedes Mal, wenn das Saxophon ausgepackt wird, ein regelmäßiger Bestandteil des Übens werden, und zwar sowohl im Studierzimmer als auch im Unterricht.

Ziel dieses Buches ist es, bereits von Anfang an diese Gewohnheit im Saxophonspiel des Schülers zu verankern. Natürlich muss man die Notennamen und Notenwerte komplett kennen und verstanden haben, aber durch das Bewusstsein für Form und Richtung wird das Vom-Blatt-Spiel gleichermaßen unterstützt.

Dieser Band hat sieben Teile, die nach und nach neue Noten, Rhythmen, Artikulation, Dynamik und italienische Begriffe in einer logischen Abfolge einführen - ganz ähnlich, wie man es in einer Schule für Anfänger auch finden würde. Der Schwerpunkt liegt auf dem Bereitstellen passender Melodien und Strukturen anstelle von sterilen Vom-Blatt-Spiel Übungen. Jeder Teil beginnt mit Solobeispielen und endet mit Duetten und begleiteten Stücken. Dadurch kann der Spieler auch Erfahrungen im Blatt-Spiel beim gemeinsamen Musizieren mit anderen machen.

Die Soli und Duette sind sowohl für Alt- als auch Tenorinstrumente geeignet. Begleitete Stücke haben Klavierstimmen für beide Instrumente.

Teil 1 beginnt mit den Noten g^1 bis h^1 und erweitert den Tonraum allmählich bis zum d^2. Das melodische Material verarbeitet hauptsächlich schrittweise Bewegungen, einfach strukturierte Phrasen sowie sich wiederholende Noten und melodische Figuren (Sequenzen).

Teil 2 hat bereits einen Tonumfang vom kleinen e^1 bis e^2 und führt das fis^1, Bindungen und Haltebögen ein.

Teil 3 erweitert den Tonumfang vom tiefen d bis g^2 und führt die Tonarten C-, G- und F-Dur ein. Außerdem werden die neuen Noten b^1 und fis^2, Achtelnoten sowie Dynamik- und Vortragszeichen vorgestellt. Die punktierte Viertelnote mit anschließender Achtelnote wird in den einfachen Taktarten 4/4, 3/4 und 2/4 eingeübt.

Teil 4 beschäftigt sich sowohl mit dem 3/8-Takt als auch mit den zusammengesetzten Taktarten 6/8, 9/8 und 12/8. Die Tonart D-Dur wird zusammen mit den neuen Noten cis^2 und a^2 vorgestellt.

Teil 5 erweitert den Tonraum noch einmal, um das gis^1 und das h^2 miteinzuschließen. Der 5/4-Takt wird vorgestellt sowie die Tonarten a-, d- und h-Moll.

Teil 6 konzentriert sich auf Synkopen und Swingrhythmen. Die Tonarten B-Dur und e-Moll kommen hinzu.

Teil 7 beschließt Band 1 mit einem Tonumfang von zwei Oktaven (c^1 bis c^3) und den Tonarten g-Moll und A-Dur.

An den Schüler: Warum Vom-Blatt-Spiel?

Wenn du dich einem neuen Musikstück gegenüber siehst und gebeten wirst, es zu spielen, egal, ob zu Hause, im Unterricht, in einem Examen oder einem Vorspiel, gibt es niemanden, der dir helfen kann – nur du selbst! Das Blatt-Spiel testet deine Fähigkeit, Taktarten und Noten richtig zu lesen, sowie Phrasierungen und Dynamik schnell zu erfassen.

Ziel dieser Ausgabe ist es, dir beim Selbstunterricht behilflich zu sein. Das Buch zeigt dir, worauf du achten sollst und wie du dich in sehr kurzer Zeit am besten vorbereitest. Das tust du, indem du dir die jeweilige Takt- und Tonart sowie den Verlauf der Melodie und die Ausdruckszeichen genau anschaust. Die kurzen Musikstücke steigern sich nur allmählich, um sowohl dein Vertrauen und deine Beobachtungsgabe aufzubauen, als auch dich dazu zu befähigen, exakt vom Blatt zu spielen. Am Ende jeden Teils stehen Duette, die du mit deinem Lehrer oder deinen Freunden spielen kannst. Außerdem gibt es Stücke mit Klavierbegleitung, die deine Fähigkeit im Blatt-Spiel überprüfen, während gleichzeitig etwas anderes abläuft. Das ist eine wesentliche Fähigkeit, wenn man mit einer Band, einem Orchester oder einer anderen Musikgruppe zusammenspielt.

Wenn du jedes Mal, wenn du Saxophon spielst, auch etwas vom Blatt spielst, wirst du überrascht sein, wie sehr du dich verbesserst. Denke daran: wenn du die meisten Melodien, die du spielen sollst, vom Blatt spielen kannst, kannst du dich auf die ‚schwierigen Teile' konzentrieren und diese viel schneller beherrschen.

Stelle dir die Melodien in diesem Band als Ministücke vor und versuche, sie schnell und korrekt zu lernen. Wenn du dann wirklich vom Blatt spielen musst, wirst du bestens ausgerüstet sein, um gleich beim ersten Versuch erfolgreich zu sein.

Jetzt bist du auf dich selbst gestellt!

Section 1 – Notes G to D
Section 1 – Notes *sol* à *si*
Teil 1 – Die Noten g¹ bis d²

Three steps to success

1. **Look at the top number of the time signature**. It shows the number of beats in a bar. Tap (or clap, sing or play on one note) the rhythm, feeling the pulse throughout. Count at least one bar of the time signature in your head to set up the pulse before you begin to tap or play each tune.

2. **Look for patterns**. While tapping the rhythm, look at the melodic shape and notice movement by step, skip, repeated notes and sequences (short, repeated melodic phrases which often rise or fall by step).

3. **Keep going**. Remember: a wrong note or rhythm can be corrected the next time you play it. If you stop, you have doubled the mistake!

Trois étapes vers la réussite

1. **Observez le chiffre supérieur de l'indication de mesure**. Il indique le nombre de pulsations contenues par mesure. Frappez (dans les mains, chantez ou jouez sur une seule note) le rythme tout en maintenant une pulsation intérieure constante. Comptez mentalement au moins une mesure complète pour installer la pulsation avant de frapper ou de jouer chaque pièce.

2. **Repérez les motifs**. Tout en frappant le rythme, observez les contours de la mélodie et relevez les mouvements par degrés conjoints, les sauts d'intervalles, les notes répétées et les séquences (courtes phrases mélodiques répétées progressant généralement par degrés ascendants ou descendants).

3. **Ne vous arrêtez pas !** Vous pourrez corriger une fausse note ou un rythme inexact la prochaine fois que vous jouerez. En vous interrompant, vous doublez la faute !

Drei Schritte zum Erfolg

1. **Schaue dir die obere Zahl der Taktangabe an**. Diese zeigt die Anzahl der Schläge in einem Takt. Schlage (klatsche, singe oder spiele auf einer Note) den Rhythmus, wobei du immer das Metrum spürst. Zähle mindestens einen Takt lang die Taktangabe im Kopf, um das Metrum zu verinnerlichen, bevor du beginnst, jede der Melodien zu klopfen oder zu spielen.

2. **Achte auf Muster**. Schaue dir die melodische Form an, während du den Rhythmus schlägst und achte auf Bewegungen in Schritten oder Sprüngen, sich wiederholende Noten und Sequenzen (kurze, sich wiederholende melodische Phrasen, die oft schrittweise ansteigen oder abfallen).

3. **Bleibe dran**. Denke daran: eine falsche Note oder ein falscher Rhythmus kann beim nächsten Mal korrigiert werden. Wenn du aber aufhörst zu spielen, verdoppelst du den Fehler!

Section 1 – Notes G to D

Section 1 – Notes *sol* à *si*

Teil 1 – Die Noten g¹ bis d²

Play at a steady speed
and with a bold tone.
Notice the melodic shapes.

Notes G to B.

Jouez à vitesse régulière et avec
hardiesse. Observez les contours
mélodiques.

Notes *sol* à *si*.

Spiele in einem gleichmäßigen
Tempo und mit einem kräftigen Ton.
Beachte die melodischen Formen.

Die Noten g¹ bis h¹.

5.

6.

Notes G to C.   Notes *sol* à *do*.   Die Noten g^2 bis c^2.

7.

Watch out for skips.   Attention aux sauts d'intervalles.   Achte auf Sprünge.

8.

9.

10.

10

Mark the shapes and patterns
with a pencil.
Notes G to D.

Soulignez les contours mélodiques
et les motifs au crayon.
Notes *sol* à *ré*.

Kennzeichne die Formen und
Muster mit einem Bleistift.
Die Noten g^1 bis d^2.

11.

12.

13.

14.

15.

16.

12

25.

ALTO / ALTO / ALT

25.

TENOR / TÉNOR / TENOR

14

26.

ALTO / ALTO / ALT

26.

TENOR / TÉNOR / TENOR

27.

ALTO / ALTO / ALT

27.

TENOR / TÉNOR / TENOR

Section 2 – Notes lower E to upper E; slurs and ties
Section 2 – Notes *mi* grave à *mi* aigu, liaisons et liaisons de phrasé
Teil 2 – Die Noten von e¹ bis e²; Bindungen und Haltebögen

Four steps to success

1. **Look at the top number of the time signature**. Tap (or clap, sing or play on one note) the rhythm, feeling the pulse throughout. Count at least one bar of the time signature in your head to set up the pulse before you begin to tap or play the tune.

2. **Look for patterns**. While tapping the rhythm, look at the melodic shape and notice movement by step, skip, repeated notes or sequences.

3. **Notice the slurring**. Often, slurring is very logical. Similar phrases will usually have the same articulation.

4. **Keep going!**

Quatre étapes vers la réussite

1. **Observez le chiffre supérieur de l'indication de mesure**. Frappez (dans les mains, chantez ou jouez sur une seule note) le rythme tout en maintenant une pulsation intérieure constante. Comptez mentalement au moins une mesure pour installer la pulsation avant de frapper ou de jouer chaque pièce.

2. **Relevez les motifs**. Tout en frappant le rythme, observez les contours de la mélodie et relevez les mouvements par degrés conjoints, les sauts d'intervalles, les notes répétées ou les séquences.

3. **Repérez les liaisons de phrasé**. Le phrasé est souvent très logique. Des phrases similaires présenteront en général la même articulation.

4. **Ne vous arrêtez pas !**

Vier Schritte zum Erfolg

1. **Schaue dir die obere Zahl der Taktangabe an**. Schlage (klatsche, singe oder spiele auf einer Note) den Rhythmus, wobei du immer das Metrum spürst. Zähle mindestens einen Takt lang die Taktangabe im Kopf, um das Metrum zu verinnerlichen, bevor du beginnst, jede der Melodien zu klopfen oder zu spielen.

2. **Achte auf Muster**. Schaue dir die melodische Form an, während du den Rhythmus schlägst und achte auf Bewegungen in Schritten oder Sprüngen, sich wiederholende Noten und Sequenzen.

3. **Konzentriere dich auf die Bindungen**. Bindungen sind oft sehr logisch. Ähnliche Phrasen haben normalerweise auch dieselbe Artikulation.

4. **Bleibe dran!**

Section 2 – Notes lower E to upper E; slurs and ties

Section 2 – Notes *mi* grave à *mi* aigu, liaisons et liaisons de phrasé

Teil 2 – Die Noten von e[1] bis e[2]; Bindungen und Haltebögen

Notice the slurs.
New note F.

Observez les liaisons de phrasé.
Nouvelle note : *fa*.

Beachte die Bindungen.
Die neue Note f[1].

18

New note F♯.   Nouvelle note : *fa*♯.   Die neue Note fis[1].

31.

32.

33.

New note upper E.   Nouvelle note : *mi* aigu.   Die neue Note e[2].

34.

35.

36.

New note lower E.　　　　　　Nouvelle note : *mi* grave.　　　　　　Die neue Note e^1.

37.

38.

39.

40.

44.

45.

46.

47.

48.

ALTO / ALTO / ALT

48.

TENOR / TÉNOR / TENOR

49.

ALTO/ALTO/ALT

49.

TENOR / TÉNOR / TENOR

50.

ALTO / ALTO / ALT

50.

TENOR / TÉNOR / TENOR

Section 3 – New keys, dynamics and performance directions; quavers and dotted crotchets

Section 3 – Nouvelles tonalités, nuances dynamiques et indications pour l'exécution ; croches et noires pointées

Teil 3 – Neue Tonarten, Dynamik- und Vortragsangaben; Achtelnoten und punktierte Viertelnoten

Five steps to success

1. **Look at the top number of the time signature**. It shows the number of beats in a bar. Tap (or clap, sing or play on one note) the rhythm, feeling the pulse throughout. Count at least one bar of the time signature in your head to set up the pulse before you begin to tap or play each tune.

2. **Look between the treble clef and the time signature for any sharps or flats**. This is known as the key signature. Make sure you know which notes these apply to and notice where they occur in the melody.

3. **Look for patterns**. While tapping the rhythm, look at the melodic shape and notice movement by step, skip, repeated notes and sequences.

4. **Look for the new dynamic marks** of f (loud) and p (quiet / gentle). Observe the dynamic shapes and notice if they change suddenly or gradually.

5. **Keep going!**

Cinq étapes vers la réussite

1. **Observez le chiffre supérieur de l'indication de mesure**. Il indique le nombre de pulsations contenues par mesure. Frappez (dans les mains, chantez ou jouez sur une seule note) le rythme tout en maintenant une pulsation intérieure constante. Comptez mentalement au moins une mesure pour installer la pulsation avant de frapper ou de jouer chaque pièce.

2. **Vérifiez les dièses ou les bémols placés entre la clef de *sol* et le chiffrage de mesure**. Ils constituent l'armure de la tonalité. Assurez-vous des notes altérées et repérez-les dans la mélodie.

3. **Repérez les motifs**. Tout en frappant le rythme, observez les contours de la mélodie et repérez les déplacements par degrés conjoints, les sauts d'intervalles, les notes répétées et les séquences.

4. **Relevez les indications de nuances** f (fort) et p (*doux*). Repérez les changements subits ou progressifs de nuances dynamiques

5. **Ne vous arrêtez pas !**

Fünf Schritte zum Erfolg

1. **Schaue dir die obere Zahl der Taktangabe an**. Diese zeigt die Anzahl der Schläge in einem Takt. Schlage (klatsche, singe oder spiele auf einer Note) den Rhythmus, wobei du immer das Metrum spürst. Zähle mindestens einen Takt lang die Taktangabe im Kopf, um das Metrum zu verinnerlichen, bevor du jede der Melodien klopfst oder spielst.

2. **Achte auf Kreuz- und B-Vorzeichen zwischen dem Notenschlüssel und der Taktangabe**. Diese bezeichnet man als Tonart. Überzeuge dich davon, dass du weißt, auf welche Noten sich diese beziehen und finde heraus, wo sie in der Melodie auftauchen.

3. **Achte auf Muster**. Schaue dir die melodische Form an, während du den Rhythmus schlägst und achte auf Bewegungen in Schritten oder Sprüngen, sich wiederholende Noten und Sequenzen.

4. **Beachte die neuen Dynamikzeichen** f (laut) und p (leise / sanft). Schaue dir die dynamischen Formen genau an und registriere, ob sie sich plötzlich oder allmählich ändern.

5. **Bleibe dran!**

Performance directions used in this section:
(You may note all directions and translations on the glossary page at the back of the book.)

Indications pour l'exécution utilisées dans cette partie :
(Vous pourrez noter toutes les indications et leur traduction sur la page de glossaire en fin de volume.)

Vortragsangaben, die in diesem Teil verwendet werden:
(Du kannst dir alle Angaben und ihre Übersetzungen im Anhang notieren.)

Allegretto	moderately fast	modérément rapide	gemäßigt schnell
Allegro	fast, quick and lively	rapide	lebhaft
Andante	at a walking pace	allant	gehend
Andantino	a little faster than Andante	un peu plus vite qu'*andante*	ein bisschen schneller als Andante
Cantabile	in a singing style	chantant	gesanglich
Con grazia	with grace	gracieusement	mit Anmut
Con moto	with movement	avec mouvement	mit Bewegung
Crescendo (*cresc.*)	gradually getting louder	de plus en plus fort	allmählich lauter werdend
Diminuendo (*dim.*)	gradually getting softer	de moins en moins fort	allmählich leiser werdend
Dolce	sweetly	doux	sanft
Giocoso	joyfully, playfully	joyeusement	scherzhaft
Leggiero	lightly	légèrement	leicht
Marcato (*marc.*)	marked / accented	marqué	markiert
Moderato	at a moderate speed	modéré	gemäßigt
Poco	a little	un peu	ein wenig
Poco a poco	little by little	peu à peu	nach und nach
Rall. (Rallentando)	gradually becoming slower	en ralentissant	allmählich langsamer werdend
Vivace	lively	vif	lebhaft

Section 3 – New keys, dynamics and performance directions; quavers and dotted crotchets

Section 3 – Nouvelles tonalités, nuances dynamiques et indications pour l'exécution ; croches et noires pointées

Teil 3 – Neue Tonarten, Dynamik- und Vortragsangaben; Achtelnoten und punktierte Viertelnoten

New note lower D.
G major.
Introducing quavers (eighth notes).

Nouvelle note : *ré* grave.
sol majeur.
Introduction des croches.

Die neue Note d[1].
G-Dur.
Die Einführung von Achtelnoten.

51.

52.

53.

Key of F major.
New note B♭.

Tonalité de *fa* majeur.
Nouvelle note : *si*♭.

Die F-Dur Tonleiter.
Die neue Note b[1].

54.

This begins on the third beat
in 3-time.
Count 1 2 3 1 2 before you begin.

Attaque sur de 3ème temps
d'une mesure à 3 temps.
Comptez 1, 2, 3, 1, 2 avant
de commencer.

Dieses Stück beginnt auf dem
dritten Schlag eines 3/4-Taktes.
Zähle 1 2 3 1 2, bevor du anfängst.

55.

New note upper F.
This begins on the fourth beat
in 4-time.
Count 1 2 3 before you begin.

Nouvelle note : *fa* aigu.
Attaque sur de 4ème temps
d'une mesure à 4 temps.
Comptez 1, 2, 3 avant
de commencer.

Die neue Note f[2].
Dieses Stück beginnt auf dem
vierten Schlag eines 4/4-Taktes.
Zähle 1 2 3, bevor du anfängst.

56.

32

This begins on the second beat in 3-time.
Count 1 2 3 1 before you begin.

Attaque sur de 2ème temps d'une mesure à 3 temps.
Comptez 1, 2, 3, 1 avant de commencer.

Dieses Stück beginnt auf dem zweiten Schlag eines 3/4-Taktes.
Zähle 1 2 3 1, bevor du anfängst.

57.

C major.
New note upper G.

do majeur.
Nouvelle note : *sol* aigu.

C-Dur.
Die neue Note g^2.

58.

This begins on the fourth beat in 4-time.
Count 1 2 3 before you begin.

Attaque sur de 4ème temps d'une mesure à 4 temps.
Comptez 1, 2, 3 avant de commencer.

Dieses Stück beginnt auf dem vierten Schlag eines 4/4-Taktes.
Zähle 1 2 3, bevor du anfängst.

59.

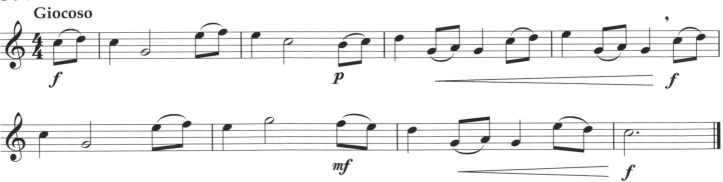

This begins on the third beat
in 3-time.
Count 1 2 3 1 2 before you begin.

Attaque sur de 3ème temps
d'une mesure à 3 temps.
Comptez 1, 2, 3, 1, 2 avant
de commencer.

Dieses Stück beginnt auf dem
dritten Schlag eines 3/4-Taktes.
Zähle 1 2 3 1 2, bevor du anfängst.

60.

New note upper F#.

Introducing ♩. ♪

Nouvelle note : fa#.

Introduction de ♩. ♪

Die neue Note fis².

Einführung von ♩. ♪

62.

63.

64.

65.

poco rall.

66.

Vivace

70. ALTO / ALTO / ALT

Con moto

70. TENOR / TÉNOR / TENOR

Con moto

71. ALTO / ALTO / ALT

Allegretto

40

71. TENOR / TÉNOR / TENOR

Allegretto

72. ALTO / ALTO / ALT

72. TENOR/TÉNOR/TENOR

Section 4 – Compound time
Section 4 – Mesures composées
Teil 4 – Zusammengesetzte Taktarten

Key steps to understanding compound rhythms

The time signatures of **6/8**, **9/8** and **12/8** are known as **compound time signatures**. Each beat is divided into three equal parts (say the word 'pineapple' to one beat) unlike simple time signatures (2/4, 3/4 and 4/4), which divide into two (say the word 'mango' to one beat).

The most common of these compound time signatures is 6/8 and means there are six equal quavers (eighth notes) in a bar. In 6/8 there are two groups of three quavers: each bar is counted in two.

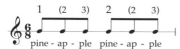

The opening two bars of 'Humpty Dumpty' contain three of the most common rhythms in compound time signatures.

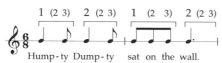

In all compound time signatures in this section,

♩. = two beats

♪. = one beat

♩ = two thirds of a beat

♪ = one third of a beat

Rappels essentiels à la compréhension des mesures composées

6/8, **9/8** et **12/8** sont des chiffrages de **mesures composées**. Chaque temps y est divisé en trois parties égales (prononcez le mot « éléphant » sur chaque temps) à la différence des mesures simples (2/4, 3/4 et 4/4) dont les temps se divisent en deux parties égales (prononcez le mot « canard » sur chaque temps).

6/8 est le chiffrage de mesure composée le plus fréquent. Il signifie que chaque mesure contient six croches égales réparties en deux groupes de trois croches. Il s'agit donc d'une mesure à deux temps.

Les deux premières mesure de *Humpty Dumpty* présentent les trois rythmes les plus souvent rencontrés dans les mesures composées.

Dans toutes les mesures composées de cette partie,

♩. = deux temps

♪. = un temps

♩ = deux tiers de temps

♪ = un tiers de temps

Die entscheidenden Schritte, um zusammengesetzte Rhythmen zu verstehen

Die Taktarten **6/8**, **9/8** und **12/8** sind als **zusammengesetzte Taktarten** bekannt. Jeder Schlag ist in drei gleichlange Teile aufgeteilt (sage das Wort *Ananas* auf einen Schlag) im Gegensatz zu einfachen Taktarten (2/4, 3/4 und 4/4), die in zwei gleichlange Teile aufgeteilt sind (sage das Wort *Mango* auf einen Schlag).

Von diesen Taktarten kommt der 6/8-Takt am häufigsten vor. Er besteht aus sechs gleichlangen Achteln pro Takt. Im 6/8-Takt gibt es zwei Gruppen mit je drei Achtelnoten: Jeder Takt hat also zwei Schläge.

Die zwei Eröffnungstakte des Kinderliedes *Humpty Dumpty* beinhalten drei der häufigsten Rhythmen, die in zusammengesetzten Taktarten vorkommen.

In allen zusammengesetzten Taktarten sind

♩. = zwei Schläge

♪. = ein Schlag

♩ = 2/3 eines Schlages

♪ = 1/3 eines Schlages

6/8 is 2 beats in a bar
(two groups of three quavers)

6/8 indique 2 temps par mesure
(deux groupes de trois croches)

Der 6/8-Takt hat 2 Schläge pro Takt
(zwei Gruppen mit drei Achteln)

9/8 is 3 beats in a bar
(three groups of three quavers)

9/8 indique 3 temps par mesure
(trois groupes de trois croches)

Der 9/8-Takt hat 3 Schläge pro Takt
(drei Gruppen mit drei Achteln)

12/8 is 4 beats in a bar
(four groups of three quavers)

12/8 indique 4 temps par mesure
(quatre groupes de trois croches)

Der 12/8-Takt hat 4 Schläge pro Takt
(vier Gruppen mit drei Achteln)

Although strictly simple time, 3/8 often takes on the characteristics of a compound time signature. It was therefore decided to include 3/8 pieces in this section.

Bien qu'appartenant aux mesures simples, la mesure à 3/8 offre souvent les même traits caratéristiques qu'une mesure composée. C'est pourquoi une pièce à 3/8 figure dans cette partie.

Obwohl er eine ganz klar einfache Taktart ist, hat der 3/8-Takt oft das Wesen einer zusammengesetzten Taktart. Daher wurde beschlossen, 3/8 Stücke in diesen Teil aufzunehmen.

Additional performance directions used in Section 4:

Nouvelles indications pour l'exécution rencontrées dans la cette partie :

Zusätzliche Vortragsangaben, die in Teil 4 vorkommen:

A tempo	return to the original speed	au mouvement original	Rückkehr zum Ausgangstempo
Con brio	with life	avec éclat	mit Leben
Espressivo	expressively	expressif	ausdrucksvoll
Molto	much	beaucoup	viel
Pesante	heavily	lourd	schwer
Poco lento	a little slowly	un peu lent	ein bisschen langsam
Rit. (Ritenuto)	holding back the time	en retenant le tempo	den Schlag verzögern

Section 4 – Compound time
Section 4 – Mesures composées
Teil 4 – Zusammengesetzte Taktarten

C major.
Count 1 (2 3) 2 (2 3)
before you begin.
Subdivide each beat into
three smaller beats.

do majeur.
Comptez 1 (2, 3) 2 (2, 3)
avant de commencer
Subdivisez chaque temps
en trois pulsations

C-Dur.
Zähle 1 (2 3) 2 (2 3),
bevor du anfängst.
Unterteile jeden Schlag
in drei kürzere Schläge.

73.

G major.

sol majeur.

G-Dur.

74.

F major.

fa majeur.

F-Dur.

75.

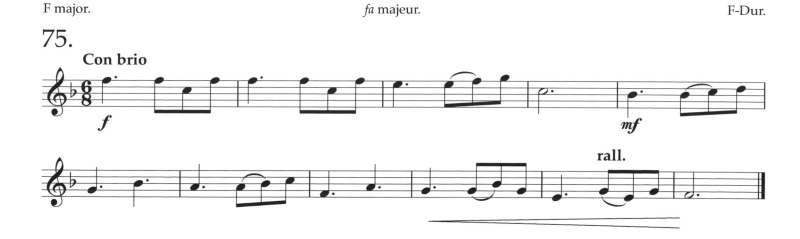

Count 1 2 3 before you begin. Comptez 1, 2, 3 avant de commencer. Zähle 1 2 3, bevor du anfängst.

76.

G major. *sol* majeur. G-Dur.

77.

C major. *do* majeur. C-Dur.
New note upper A. Nouvelle note : *la* aigu. Die neue Note a^2.

78.

G major. *sol* majeur. G-Dur.
Count 1 2 3 4 before you begin. Comptez 1, 2, 3, 4 avant de commencer. Zähle 1 2 3 4, bevor du anfängst.

79.

D major.
New note C#.

ré majeur.
Nouvelle note : *do*#.

D-Dur.
Die neue Note cis^2.

80.

Moderato

Count 1 (2 3) before you begin.

Comptez 1 (2, 3) avant de commencer.

Zähle 1 (2 3), bevor du anfängst.

81.

Con moto

G major.
Watch out for accidentals.

sol majeur.
Attention aux
altérations accidentelles.

G-Dur
Achte auf Vorzeichen
innerhalb des Stückes.

82.

Vivace

83.

84.

85.

86.

87. ALTO / ALTO / ALT

Andante

87. TENOR/TÉNOR/TENOR

88. ALTO / ALTO / ALT

Andante espressivo

88.
TENOR / TÉNOR / TENOR

Andante espressivo

89. ALTO/ALTO/ALT

Poco lento

89. TENOR / TÉNOR / TENOR

Poco lento

Section 5 – Extending the range, 5/4-time and minor keys

Section 5 – Extension de la tessiture, mesure à 5/4 et tonalités mineures

Teil 5 – Ausdehnung des Tonraumes, 5/4-Takt und Molltonarten

Six steps to success

1. **Look at the time signature**. Tap (or clap, sing or play on one note) the rhythm, feeling the pulse throughout. Count at least one bar of the time signature in your head to set up the pulse before you begin to tap or play each tune.

2. **Look between the treble clef and the time signature for any sharps or flats**. Make sure you know which notes these apply to and notice where they occur in the melody. Sort out the fingerings before you begin.

3. **Look out for accidentals**. Check that you know the fingerings before you arrive at the note.

4. **Look for patterns**. While tapping the rhythm, look at the melodic shape and notice movement by step, skip, repeated notes and sequences.

5. **Notice the articulations and dynamics**.

6. **Keep going!**

Six étapes vers la réussite

1. **Observez le chiffrage de mesure**. Frappez (dans les mains, chantez ou jouez sur une seule note) le rythme tout en maintenant une pulsation intérieure constante. Comptez mentalement au moins une mesure pour installer la pulsation avant de frapper ou de jouer chaque pièce.

2. **Vérifiez l'armure de la tonalité placée entre la clef de *sol* et le chiffrage de mesure**. Assurez-vous des notes altérées et repérez-les dans la mélodie. Prévoyez les doigtés avant d'attaquer.

3. **Recherchez les altérations accidentelles**. Vérifiez-en le doigté avant de les atteindre.

4. **Repérez les motifs**. Tout en frappant le rythme, observez les contours de la mélodie et relevez les déplacements par degrés conjoints, les sauts d'intervalles, les notes répétées et les séquences.

5. **Observez les phrasés et les nuances**.

6. **Ne vous arrêtez pas !**

Sechs Schritte zum Erfolg

1. **Schaue dir die Taktangabe an**. Schlage (klatsche, singe oder spiele auf einer Note) den Rhythmus, wobei du immer das Metrum spürst. Zähle mindestens einen Takt lang die Taktangabe im Kopf, um das Metrum zu verinnerlichen, bevor du beginnst, jede der Melodien zu klopfen oder zu spielen.

2. **Achte auf Kreuz- und B-Vorzeichen zwischen dem Notenschlüssel und der Taktangabe**. Versichere dich, dass du weißt, auf welche Noten sich diese beziehen und finde heraus, wo in der Melodie sie auftauchen. Überprüfe ihre Griffweise, bevor du zu spielen anfängst.

3. **Suche nach Notenvorzeichen**. Stelle sicher, dass du die Griffweise kennst, bevor du diese Note erreichst.

4. **Achte auf Muster**. Schaue dir die melodische Form an, während du den Rhythmus schlägst und achte auf Bewegungen in Schritten oder Sprüngen, sich wiederholende Noten und Sequenzen.

5. **Beachte Artikulation und Dynamik**.

6. **Bleibe dran!**

Additional performance directions used in this section:

Nouvelles indications pour l'exécution rencontrées dans cette partie :

Zusätzliche Vortragsangaben, die in Teil 5 benutzt werden:

Dolce sostenuto	sweetly and sustained	doux et soutenu	süß und zurückhaltend
Maestoso	majestically	majestueux	majestätisch
March	in a military style	marche militaire	in militärischem Stil

Section 5 – Extending the range, 5/4-time and minor keys

Section 5 – Extension de la tessiture, mesure à 5/4 et tonalités mineures

Teil 5 – Ausdehnung des Tonraumes, 5/4-Takt und Molltonarten

C major.   *do* majeur.   C-Dur.

90.

A minor.   *la* mineur.   a-Moll.
Introducing upper G♯   Introduction de *sol*♯ aigu et grave.   Einführung des gis[1]
and lower G♯.   Comptez 1, 2, 1 avant de commencer.   und des gis[2].
Count 1 2 1 before you begin.   Zähle 1 2 1, bevor du anfängst.

91.

92.

58

Introducing 5-time.
Count 1 2 3 4 5 before you begin.

Introduction de la mesure à 5 temps.
Comptez 1, 2, 3, 4, 5
avant de commencer.

Einführung des 5/4-Taktes.
Zähle 1 2 3 4 5,
bevor du anfängst.

93.

F major.

fa majeur.

F-Dur.

94.

D minor.
Introducing upper B♭.
This begins on the fourth
beat in 4-time.
Count 1 2 3 before you begin.

ré mineur.
Introduction de *si*♭ aigu
Attaque sur le 4ème temps
d'une mesure à 4 temps.
Comptez 1, 2, 3 avant de commencer.

d-Moll
Einführung des b².
Dieses Stück beginnt auf dem
vierten Schlag eines 4/4-Taktes.
Zähle 1 2 3, bevor du anfängst.

95.

96.

D major.   *ré* majeur.   D-Dur.

97.

98.

B minor.   *si* mineur.   h-Moll.

99.

100.

101.

102.

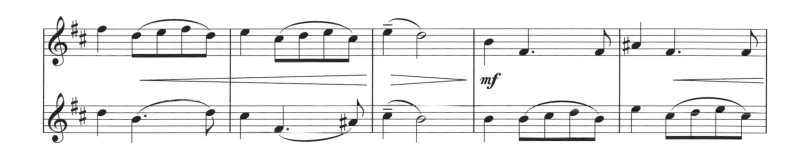

103.

104.

Allegro

105.

ALTO / ALTO / ALT

Con moto

105.

TENOR / TÉNOR / TENOR

Con moto

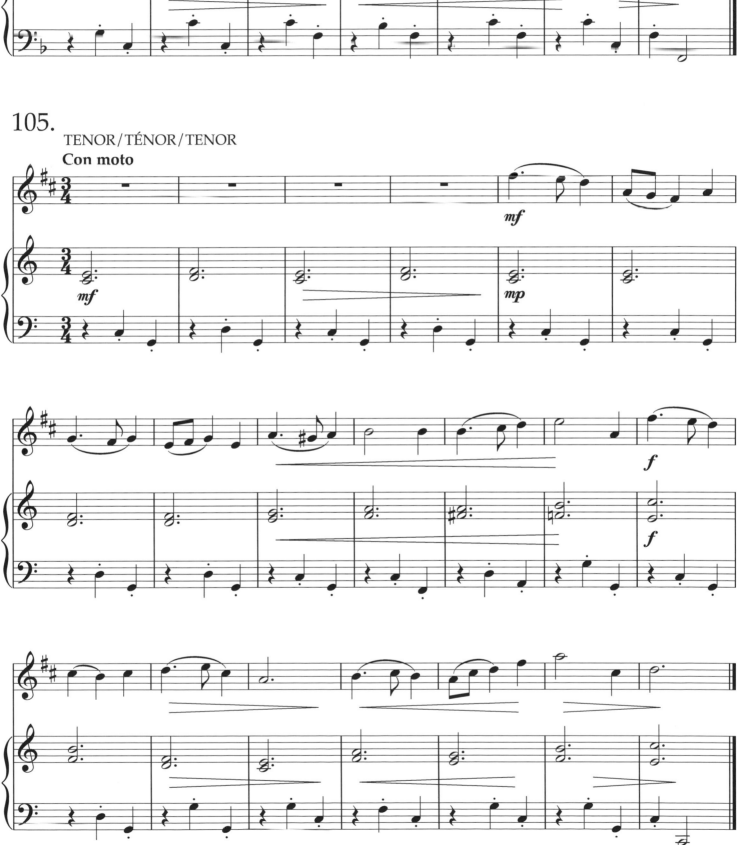

106. ALTO / ALTO / ALT

Dolce sostenuto

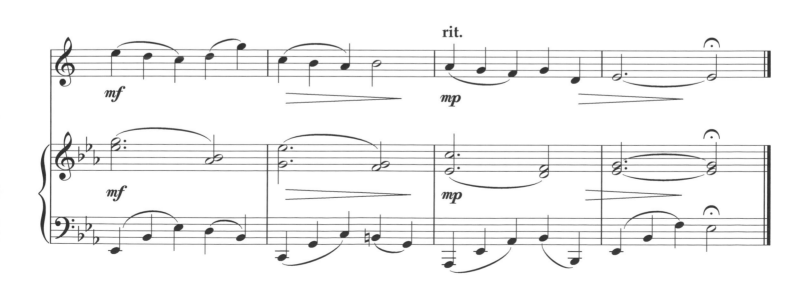

106. TENOR/TÉNOR/TENOR

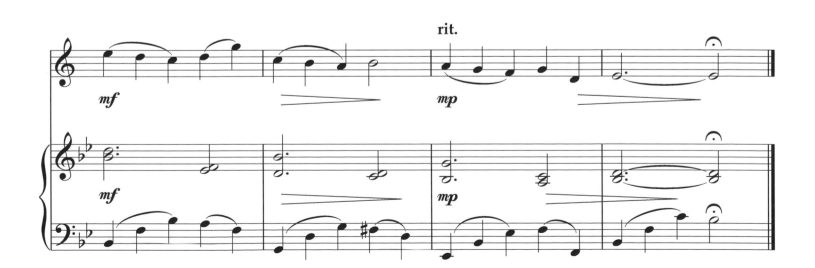

107. ALTO / ALTO / ALT

Lazily

Nonchalamment / träge

107.

TENOR/TÉNOR/TENOR

Lazily

Nonchalamment/träge

Section 6 – Syncopations and swing rhythms; new keys of B♭ major and E minor

Section 6 – Syncopes et rythmique *swing*, tonalités de *si*♭ majeur et de *mi* mineur

Teil 6 – Synkopen und Swingrhythmen; die neuen Tonarten B-Dur und e-Moll

Syncopation is the displacement of either the beat or the normal accent of a piece of music. Syncopation has been a vital element in jazz and popular music since the 1890s and the beginning of ragtime. In simple terms, ♩ ♫ and ♫ ♩ are replaced by ♪♩ ♪

Swing rhythms

Swing rhythms are what most people think of as 'jazz', with its easily recognisable relaxed triplet feel. Jazz grew out of ragtime and spirituals in the early 20th century.

There are many forms of jazz: Dixieland, blues, traditional, swing, bebop and many others. Common to most is a flexible notation born out of the fact that jazz is mostly an aural tradition. Interpreting 'jazz quavers' (eighth notes) is a focus for this section.

Jazz quavers may be notated in two ways:

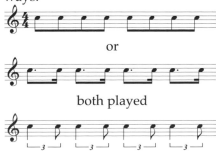

or

both played

La syncope est le déplacement soit de la pulsation rythmique soit de l'accentuation normale de la musique. C'est une composante essentielle du jazz et de la musique populaire depuis les année 1890 et les débuts du *ragtime*. Pour simplifier ♩ ♫ et ♫ ♩ sont remplacés par ♪♩ ♪

Rythmes *swing*

La rythmique *swing* est communé-ment associée au jazz et est facilement reconnaissable à son allure ternaire libre. Le jazz se développa à partir du *ragtime* et des spirituals au début du XXème siècle.

Il existe de nombreuses formes de jazz dont, entre autres, le *dixieland*, le *blues*, le jazz classique, le *swing*, le *be bop*. Tous ces styles ont en commun une notation souple due à la transmission traditionnellement orale du jazz. Cette partie se concentre sur l'interprétation de « croches jazz »

Les croches jazz sont notées de deux façons :

ou :

toutes deux joués ainsi :

Synkopen sind die Verschiebung des Schlages oder der normalen Betonung eines Musikstückes. Synkopen sind seit den 1890er Jahren und dem Beginn des Ragtime ein bedeutendes Element im Jazz und der Popularmusik. Einfach ausgedrückt: ♩ ♫ und ♫ ♩ werden durch ♪♩ ♪ ersetzt.

Swingrhythmen

Swingrhythmen sind das, was die meisten Leute unter ‚Jazz' verstehen, mit seinem leicht wiederzuerken-nenden, entspannten Triolengefühl. Der Jazz entwickelte sich aus dem Ragtime und den Spirituals des frühen 20. Jahrhunderts.

Es gibt viele Formen des Jazz: Diexieland, Blues, Swing, Bebop und viele andere. Allen gemeinsam ist eine flexible Notation, die dem Umstand entspringt, dass der Jazz eine fast ausschließlich akustische Tradition besitzt. Das Interpretieren von ‚Jazzachteln' ist der Hauptschwerpunkt dieses Teils.

Jazzachtel kann man auf zwei Arten notieren:

oder:

Beide werden wie folgt gespielt:

Additional performance directions used in this section:

Nouvelles indications pour l'exécution rentrées dans cette partie :

Zusätzliche Vortragsangaben, die in diesem Teil benutzt werden:

Non troppo	not too much	pas trop	nicht zu viel
Risoluto	resolutely	résolu	entschieden
Ritmico	rhythmically	rythmé	rhythmisch
Vivo	lively	vif/rapide	lebendig

Section 6 – Syncopations and swing rhythms; new keys of B♭ major and E minor

Section 6 – Syncopes et rythmique *swing*, tonalités de *si*♭ majeur et de *mi* mineur

Teil 6 – Synkopen und Swingrhythmen; die neuen Tonarten B-Dur und e-Moll

108.

New note D♯.   Nouvelle note : *ré*♯.   Die neue Note dis².

109.

110.

111.

112.

E minor. *mi* mineur. e-Moll.

113.

Vivace

114.

Allegretto

115.

Giocoso

116.

Ritmico

117.

Andante moderato

118.

B♭ major.   *si*♭ majeur.   B-Dur.

119.

120.

121.

Bright swing tempo

Tempo de *swing* brillant / fröhliches Swingtempo

122.

Heavy blues tempo

Tempo de *blues* lourd / Schweres Bluestempo

123.

Bright jazz waltz

Valse jazz brillante / fröhlicher Jazzwalzer

124.

Wistful jazz waltz

Valse jazz nostalgique / Wehmütiger Jazzwalzer

125.

Risoluto (even quavers)

(croches égales) / (gleichmäßige Achtelnoten)

126.

Andante (even quavers)
(croches égales) / (gleichmäßige Achtelnoten)

127.

Vivace

128.

Con brio (swing quavers ♫ = ♩♪)
(croches *swing*)/(Swingachtelnoten)

129.

Moderate blues tempo ♫ = ♩♪
Tempo de *blues* modéré / gemäßigtes Bluestempo

130. ALTO / ALTO / ALT
Allegro moderato (straight quavers)
(croches égales) / (gleichmäßige Achtelnoten)

130. TENOR/TÉNOR/TENOR

Allegro moderato (straight quavers)
(croches égales)/(gleichmäßige Achtelnoten)

131. ALTO/ALTO/ALT

Moderate jazz waltz

Valse jazz modéré/gemäßigter Jazzwalzer

131.

TENOR / TÉNOR / TENOR

Moderate jazz waltz

Valse jazz modéré / gemäßigter Jazzwalzer

132. ALTO/ALTO/ALT

Fast swing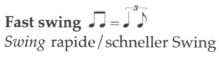
Swing rapide/schneller Swing

132. TENOR/TÉNOR/TENOR

Section 7 – Extending the range to two octaves (lower C to upper C); G minor and A major

Section 7 – Extension de la tessiture à deux octaves (*do* grave à *do* aigu), tonalités de *sol* mineur et de *la* majeur

Teil 7 – Der Tonumfang wird auf zwei Oktaven ausgedehnt (c¹ bis c³); g-Moll und A-Dur

Reading at sight: giving a musical performance

1. Look at the **time signature**. Tap (or clap, sing or play on one note) the rhythm, feeling the pulse throughout. Count at least one bar in your head before you begin to play.

2. Look at the **key signature**. Identify which notes the sharps and flats apply to. Also look for **accidentals** in the piece and work out the fingerings.

3. Look for **patterns**. While tapping the rhythm, look at the melodic shape and notice movement by step, skip, repeated notes and sequences.

4. Observe the **articulations** and **dynamics**.

5. Aim to give a **musical performance** of each piece. Before you begin to play, observe the character of the music given in the performance direction. Look ahead while playing, and keep going.

Performance directions introduced in this section:

La lecture à vue est d'abord une interprétation musicale

1. Observez le **chiffrage de mesure**. Frappez (dans les mains, chantez ou jouez sur une seule note) le rythme tout en maintenant une pulsation intérieure constante. Comptez mentalement au moins une mesure avant d'attaquer.

2. Vérifiez l'**armure de la tonalité** et à quelles notes s'appliquent les altérations. Repérez les **altérations accidentelles** survenant en cours du morceau et prévoyez-en les doigtés.

3. Repérez **les motifs**. Tout en frappant les rythmes, observez les contours de la mélodie et relevez les déplacements par degrés conjoints, les sauts d'intervalles, les notes répétées et les séquences.

4. Respectez les **phrasés** et les **nuances**.

5. Recherchez la **musicalité**. Avant d'attaquer, imprégnez-vous du caractère du morceau en vous aidant des indications pour l'exécution. Lisez à l'avance pendant que vous jouez et ne vous arrêtez pas.

Nouvelles indications d'exécution rencontrées dans cette partie :

Vom Blatt spielen: eine musikalische Darbietung geben

1. Achte auf die **Taktart**. Schlage (oder klatsche, singe oder spiele auf einer Note) den Rhythmus, wobei du immer das Metrum spürst. Zähle mindestens einen Takt lang die Taktangabe im Kopf, bevor du zu spielen beginnst.

2. Achte auf die **Tonart**. Identifiziere die Noten, zu denen die Kreuze und Bs gehören. Schaue auch nach Vorzeichen innerhalb des Stückes und überlege dir einen Fingersatz.

3. Achte auf **Muster**. Schaue dir die melodische Form an, während du den Rhythmus schlägst und achte auf Bewegungen in Schritten oder Sprüngen, sich wiederholende Noten und Sequenzen.

4. Beachte **Artikulation** und **Dynamik**.

5. Bemühe dich um eine **musikalische Darbietung** eines jeden Stückes. Bevor du zu spielen beginnst, beachte den Charakter der Musik, der durch die Vortragsangaben angezeigt wird. Schaue beim Spielen voraus und bleibe dran.

Vortragsangaben, die in diesem Teil vorgestellt werden:

Alla marcia	in the style of a march	en style de marche	im Marschstil
Calypso	a style of song from Trinidad	style de chanson originaire de Trinidad	der Stil eines Liedes aus Trinidad
Con spirito	with spirit	avec esprit	mit Geist
Grazioso	gracefully	gracieux	anmutig
Scherzando	in a playful style	en badinant	auf spielerische Art und Weise

Section 7 – Extending the range to two octaves (lower C to upper C); G minor and A major

Section 7 – Extension de la tessiture à deux octaves (*do* grave à *do* aigu), tonalités de *sol* mineur et de *la* majeur

Teil 7 – Der Tonumfang wird auf zwei Oktaven ausgedehnt (c¹ bis c³); g-Moll und A-Dur

New notes upper B and upper C.   Nouvelles notes: *si* aigu et *do* aigu.   Die neuen Noten h² und c³.

133.

New note lower C.   Nouvelle note : *do* grave.   Die neue Note c¹.

134.

135.

Moderato e scherzando

136.

Calypso

137.

Grazioso

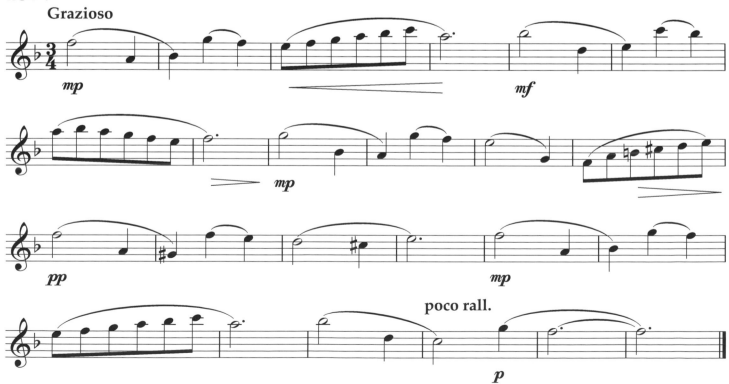

138.

139.

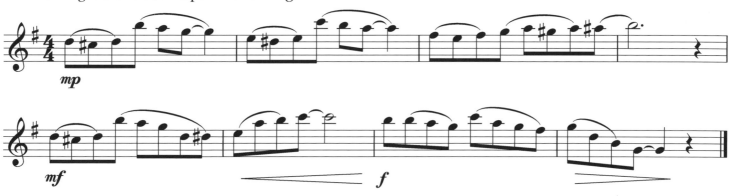

140.

G minor.   *sol* mineur.   g-Moll.

141.

142.

143.

144.

Con spirito

145.

Moderate swing

Swing modéré / gemäßigter Swing

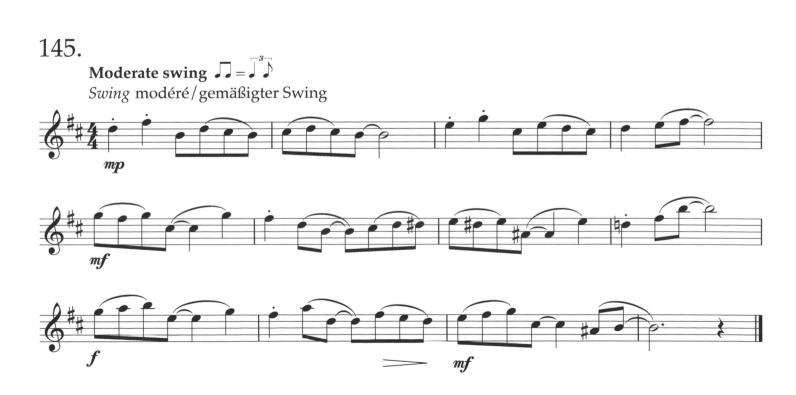

146.

Bright jazz waltz

Valse jazz brillante / fröhlicher Jazzwalzer

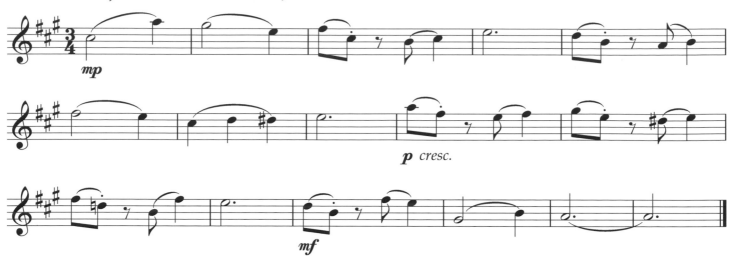

147.

Allegretto

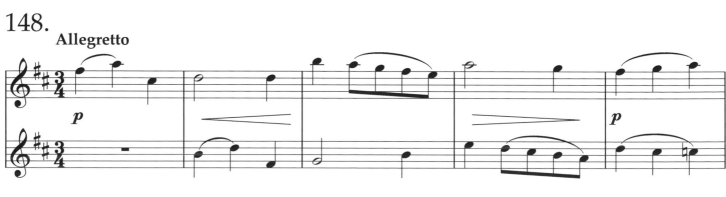

148.

Allegretto

149.

Allegro

150.

152.

ALTO/ALTO/ALT

Jazz waltz

Valse jazz/Jazzwalzer

152. TENOR / TÉNOR / TENOR

Jazz waltz ♫ = ♪ ♪
Valse jazz / Jazzwalzer

153. ALTO / ALTO / ALT

Moderato

153. TENOR/TÉNOR/TENOR

Moderato

98

154.

ALTO / ALTO / ALT

Bright swing

Swing brillant / fröhlicher Swing

154.

TENOR/TÉNOR/TENOR

Bright swing ♪♪ = ♪♪♪

Swing brillant/fröhlicher Swing

Glossary
Glossaire
Glossar

Note performance directions together with their translations used throughout the book so that you have a complete list. Writing them down will help you to remember them.

Inscrivez ici les indications d'exécution utilisées dans ce volume et leur traduction pour en établir une liste complète. Le fait de les noter vous aidera à les retenir.

Schreibe hier alle Vortragsangaben, die in diesem Band verwendet werden, zusammen mit ihren Übersetzungen auf, so dass du eine vollständige Liste hast. Das Aufschreiben wird dir dabei helfen sie einzuprägen.

Adagio	Slowly	Lent	Langsam